SNOW STOPPED PLAY

SNOW STOPPED PLAY

The Mysterious World of the Cricket Ground in Winter

GRAHAM COSTER

SAFE**H**AVEN

First published 2015 by
Safe Haven Books Ltd
12 Chinnocks Wharf
42 Narrow Street
London E14 8DJ

www.safehavenbooks.co.uk

A catalogue record for this book is available from the British Library.

ISBN 978 0 9932911 0 4

10 9 8 7 6 5 4 3 2 1

2019 2018 2017 2016 2015

The Safe Haven team on *Snow Stopped Play*:
Graham Coster, Ashley Western, Caroline Buckland, David Welch,
Andrew Treip, Graham Eames

Designed by Ashley Western in Brandon and Bell

Printed and bound in China by Everbest

CONTENTS

INTRODUCTION

The swallows are back. At the Nevill Ground, when Kent visit Tunbridge Wells in June, the rhododendrons will be swathed pink behind the bowler's arm. Leave your stripy deckchair at Hove during the luncheon interval and stroll down to the seafront, and there will be sunbathers basking on the beach. Cross over Scarborough's North Marine Road in August, and beyond the cliff down in North Bay you'll see kiddies attacking the sand with bucket and spade or even frolicking in the sea.

This is when we play – and watch – cricket. It's the Summer Game. Pavilions bedizened with hanging baskets; please cover your car windscreen so the sun's reflection doesn't blind the batsman; another pint of Pedigree under a shady marquee – why not?

And that's the point. The best game of all is played at the best time of year, when the grass is greenest, the sky is bluest, and the sun is hottest. Everything buds and blooms and beams with the cricket season: the birds, the trees, the plants, the sun, the heart. And, like the swallows, it doesn't stay very long: cricket arrives in April, and come September it's gone, and then we're back in the not-cricket bit of the year. Now we just have to wait for everything to get darker, and colder, and drearier, for months and months, before it'll come back, and we can go back to places like Lord's, or Arundel, or Canterbury, or Aigburth again.

But of course these places don't disappear, even if the game itself does. They're as bound by the seasons as everything else. Winter falls. The sky turns to porridge, and soon it feels cold

enough to... And one morning we wake up to find the bedroom window a swirl of white, and outside the world has become a hushed, bleached kingdom of sparkling snow.

So what is it that is so mesmerising, so numinous, about a cricket ground in winter? Why should something that reminds us so precisely of what we're missing, of what we can't watch for months, turn out nevertheless to arrest our gaze? And how is it that, in a perverse, counter-intuitive way, a cricket ground in winter, deserted, temporarily abandoned by the game itself, seems still to make us think so much, and tell us so much, about the beauty and inscrutability of the game of cricket?

This small book seeks to ponder such questions: questions so profoundly esoteric and peripheral that no-one appears ever to have asked them before. Among its pages you will see scarcely a ball bowled, or a stroke played. Nor will you see a single wicket – not even a leaf – fall. In certain images the evidence that there is even a cricket ground there at all will be miraculously rudimentary. It isn't even published during the cricket season, but, as it has to be, in anticipation of the dead of winter. By all means save it for a slow, baking afternoon and a dead wicket at Northampton, but it will be a long wait.

GRAHAM COSTER, MAY 2015

CRICKET WHITES

Cricket wears white. Isn't this the message from the home of cricket? This is a game that is meant to be played in white: that's what differentiates it from every other sport except tennis, and then only at Wimbledon. There's a civility in white; a crispness; a concentration – even a purity. It's why we wear white shirts for serious work, and (if we're women) with our wedding dresses.

Do you remember the first-ever World Cup Final, here at this ground on a blazingly sunny day back in 1975? The greatest cricket match he'd ever umpired, in Dickie Bird's opinion. Clive Lloyd, the West Indies captain, coming in to join Rohan Kanhai, and soon Dennis Lillee, Jeff Thomson, Max Walker and Gary Gilmour, some of the best pace bowlers in the world, were watching their good-length balls cracked to the boundary in flashing cover drives, or simply hammered back past them like "a man knocking a thistle-top off with his walking stick", in John Arlott's felicitous phrase. Kanhai, hitherto becalmed, had become inspired to cut loose too, and 40 years later the BBC video is still electrifying to watch. "This has not been a question of slogging," says Jim Laker in his television commentary, as Lloyd brings up his hundred in just 85 balls, the finest I've ever seen, and Lord's rises to him. "This has been a question of beautiful, cultured strokeplay." The crowd is raucous, bulging and spilling over the boundary ropes; the players are in white.

And why is Lord's, in this sun-dazzled winter view, entirely white? Because the MCC chose white seats for every row in every stand, and quite right too. Don't those white-clad players in County Championship, Test and club matches make you see the greenness of the grass and the blueness of the sky – even the game itself – more intensely? If you work too hard on a painting you can end up spoiling it: why throw on so much colour that nothing stands out?

A HUSH FALLS

One of our top cricket photographers, Graham Morris is at every Test match capturing split-second slip catches and bats raised to standing ovations – but every time it snows properly in London ("which is rare these days") he makes a point of heading to Lord's to take a picture. This – the last time it happened – was in 2007.

When you think of his day job, you understand why. Here is a vision of stillness and peace to balance the hubbub and roar of a Test match. Look at the seats frosted with, the handrails upholstered with, soft snow like white plush, and the playing surface a luminously unblemished carpet.

But I wonder too if this picture reminds us that a deep hush is also a part of the game of cricket itself: that moment as a departing Botham disappears into the pavilion after a century cheered to the rafters, or the moment of anticipation before Keith Miller emerges from the Long Room to run down the steps and stride swishing his bat to the wicket…

AIRSHIP AT THE NURSERY END

Philip Brown, another of our top cricket photographers, couldn't resist this shot of Lord's on another radiant winter's day. But here the whiteness, rather than encouraging us to listen, turns Lord's greyscale: makes us look spatially. With no colours to distract the eye (in contrast to the Caribbean blue sky), we notice the shapes and textures. That media centre no longer seems like an alien spacecraft: it's like the ground's benign eye. I hadn't noticed that little pod underneath before: if it looks like anything, indeed, it's a rather square airship moored at the Nursery End.

The fall of snow makes us scrutinise the overall architecture of the ground: the pleasing serration of the rows of seats in the Edrich stand; the flagpole surmounting the Grandstand like the rigging-draped mast on the Royal yacht *Britannia*; all the stands gently reclining from the playing area, not hunched and towering over it – still a cricket ground, not a stadium.

PARABOLAS

A cricket ground transformed into pure geometry. All I know is that it's somewhere in Kent. Nature's exercise in abstraction shows us the least a cricket ground can be reduced to and still be recognisable – although of course the "square" is no longer a square, but a cat's cradle of billowing parabolas in line and shadow. Note how the snow settled on the far rope catches the light to draw it in a purer white.

❋ From a square turned into curves to a cricket ground turned into black lines. This Mayan terracing is in Luton.

RACHEL WHITEREAD'S PAVILION

A less quaint and bucolic pavilion than Worcester's you could not conceive – this is Hadleigh and Thundersley CC in Essex. Note the stainless steel receptacle affixed to the wall to stub your fags out on, and what appears to be an itinerant traffic cone that the snow has almost transformed into a miniature Christmas tree. Architecturally it would look more at home as the commentary box on a minor motor-racing circuit, or even somewhere on a trading estate you'd go to for some secondhand tyres. And yet, doesn't the whiteness of the snowscape turn it into a cousin of Rachel Whiteread's "House": all textured surfaces and irregular planes and inside-out recesses – a plaster-cast of another building that has since been peeled away?

EXTRA-TERRESTRIAL

Now the mothership really has landed from a distant nebula, and in London SE11. This is indeed the Oval, and as a giant shadow has darkened the Kennington Park Road and the craft has settled next to the Tube station, the gunmetal clamshell of the fuselage has parted to reveal… a vast communion wafer, bigger than gasholders – bigger than whole parks…

❄ From this angle that Oval spaceship appears to be some kind of cousin to the craft in *2001: A Space Odyssey* – a great hollow wheel that must have gyrated through the heavens to find our small teeming planet.

PRE-SEASON

Not much is written about pre-season training, and perhaps for very good reason. Even those *Diary of a Season* books that people like Bob Willis and Brian Brain used to write start with the first match, and then grumble merely about the cold and the rain. Nowadays, of course, pre-season training starts in November, just seven weeks after the end of the previous season, for weight-training and even "combat sessions": not so long ago you reported for nets and a bit of running a week or two before the first game, with John Emburey coining the motto that "If you ain't got muscles, you can't pull them."

Here are Yorkshire, then, turning up for first practice just in time for snow in April. On the left are opening pair Stott and Taylor at Headingley in 1961, and on the right, at Bradford Park Avenue on 14 April 1966, that is indeed a bespectacled Geoffrey Boycott, with Don Wilson and Jimmy Binks – these days the first Championship matches are already taking place by that date, which says something about global warming as well as the length of the season. A few weeks earlier he'd been batting out in Australia. I'm sure he much prefers spending April under his wide-brimmed Panama out in the Caribbean with *Test Match Special*.

BAT OR BOWL FIRST?

By 1999, and a day earlier in the year than Boycott and his colleagues were turning up for net practice, the first-class cricket season was already starting. Up at Chester-le-Street, however, Durham's wasn't, with the first day of their opening match against Worcestershire wiped out by an inch of snow. Following an inspection of the pitch, captain David Boon ponders whether this would be a good toss to win or lose. A wicket of uneven bounce sees Steve Harmison getting his hoick to Cow Corner a little high on the bat. Paul Collingwood keeps wicket.

❋ Would a red ball or a pink one stand out best against the outfield?

TRACKS

Statistically it is more likely to snow at Easter time than at Christmas –
something to do with the slow rate at which the world's oceans warm up.
Easter can be as early as 25 March, and as late as 25 April, which means
well into the cricket season.

It snowed at Edgbaston at the end of March in 2013, and here the
groundstaff are trying to sweep the snow off the covers on the square.
Somehow the main action, however, is that mysterious pattern of tracks left
by the tractor in the foreground. (It must have been something motorised
and rideable, and not the green barrow we can see beside the wicket cover,
because there is not a single footprint to be seen.) What I want to know is:
why did it advance at all into that pristine expanse of white towards the
pavilion end – and then just stop? And how did it manage to reverse again
along precisely the same tracks? Or did it just dematerialise into thin air?

❋ For the final first-class match by the great Doctor, Surrey's opening game of the season against the Gentlemen of England, a bumper bank holiday crowd was expected on Easter Monday 1908. But it snowed on WG's parade...

FIRST CLASS CRICKET IN A SNOWSTORM AT KENNINGTON OVAL.

During the opening cricket match of the season between Surrey and the Gentlemen of England, played yesterday in bitterly cold weather, at Kennington Oval, a blinding snowstorm at one time actually drove the players from the field for half an hour. (1) Spectators watching the game in a snowstorm. (2) Dr. W. G. Grace leads the Gentlemen of England from the pavilion.—(Half-Tones.)

MUSH

The snow that had first fallen at Edgbaston in pre-season in 2013 was still lingering in April in congealed remnants for Warwickshire's opening match. Here is almost the same view as in the earlier picture – just from ground level. Barely a sprinkling of spectators; floodlights already on, not because the day is waning, it appears, but because that mushroom sky is not letting any light through. Even the snow, sooty and drab, is unedifying. Probably a wise call for the players to come off, and an excellent argument for Warwickshire to resuscitate their Stratford-upon-Avon festival in high summer.

THE SNOWFLAKE ON JOHN ARLOTT'S SLEEVE

Warwickshire had been snowed upon eight years earlier, too, when a sudden fall interrupted the 2005 season-opener at Lord's between MCC and the county champions. Nick Knight seems a little disappointed that George Sharp the umpire is uprooting the stumps and his innings, but the MCC fielders have already turned for the pavilion.

In 1975 John Arlott maintained that snow had fallen at Lord's as late as June during the match between Middlesex and Surrey: strolling from the pavilion to the press box he'd noticed snowflakes on his jacket sleeve, and in his match report for the *Manchester Guardian* he went as far as to describe the fall as "fairly steady".

The claim triggered a letter from an S. Gomez, who had been at the game and seen nothing but rain. The *Guardian* neglected to print it. Then the BBC World Service picked up the story, and before Mr Gomez knew it, the fact that snow had fallen at Lord's in June had been broadcast around the globe. Now he was really angry, and left with no option but to make a full-blown complaint to the British Press Council.

The five-month consideration of the matter – resumed at the greatest length, for some reason, in the *Milwaukee Journal* – included a four-page testimonial by Arlott's editor, Geoffrey Taylor, submitting that, just as it only took one black swan to disprove the notion that all swans are white, so if Arlott had seen but one snowflake on his sleeve, then there had been snow. Complaint disallowed. Arlott dismissed the controversy as "a snowstorm in a teacup."

"S. Gomez" turned out to be the nom-de-plume of Laurie Weidberg, "a socialist eccentric, infuriatingly rude and dogmatic", according to his obituary, who apparently sustained his campaign against Arlott's misinformation until his death in 1986, and died hating "the *Guardian* newspaper and its soggy bourgeois

liberalism". Almost 40 years on, the issue was still under discussion, and a brief flurry of correspondence in the *Guardian* in 2014 came to Arlott's rescue. Geoff Jackson from Langley-on-Tyne offered his "eccentric but truthful memory that it also snowed in Northumberland that day. Driving ewes and lambs through a late morning's snow squall close to that switchback of a B6318 above Corbridge was memorable." David Critchlow of Poole recalled how an aunt used to send him old newspapers for the date of his birthday, 4 August, with one from around the time of the war including a picture of women at Victoria station heading for Glyndebourne clad in fur coats against the snow down in Sussex. Eileen Bower of Huddersfield wrote of two elderly cousins "who had lived all their lives on a remote hill farm on the fells near Bewcastle, telling us that they had seen snow lying on the ground in every month except July".

TREES

Trees make a cricket ground, as we see in this fabulous view of the Parks, Oxford University's cricket ground. Remember the lovely shady avenue of trees by which you approached Kent's St Lawrence Ground – before they all went to make way for that Sainsbury's convenience store? And the view from the pavilion at the Rose Bowl of that sea of forest beyond… until that hotel was plonked in front to block them out?

At the height of summer, beautiful bucolic grounds like the Walker Ground at Southgate, Arundel Castle, and especially Coldharbour in the Surrey Hills, are more like woodland clearings. And yet it's precisely then that we don't look at the trees, but see them simply as a green curtain pulled round the boundary.

In winter, though, as David Hockney has demonstrated in his rapturous paintings of trees in the Yorkshire Wolds, we see their architecture. We sense skeletons in finest filigree; the tendrils at every bough's fingertips; even the loadbearing physics of their branch structure, the strength that sags under snow that also sustains the weight of those thousands of leaves.

FROSTY FOREST

We tend to remember – and memorialise – trees individually, and cricket trees too. It is the lone specimen that stands apart like a statue – this April I noticed for the first time the magnolia outside the club shop at Hove, because it had burst into voluptuous pink blossom to greet the first home game of the season. But, as Roger Deakin, the author of that masterpiece about wild swimming, *Waterlog*, used to maintain, trees are herd animals. It's why we have woods, and forests, and copses, and hangers.

Here is just such a herd peacefully jostling the boundary at Sevenoaks. Once the leaves come in spring they'll have coalesced into the woods beyond.

THE KENT LIME

This is the St Lawrence Ground in Canterbury, and its lime tree: not, however, The Lime Tree, which had stood sentinel in the deep at the Nackington Road end, 90 feet high, one of only two trees inside a cricket field's boundary, until 2005 when high winds broke it in two.

In winter its replacement looks as nude and spindly as a newly-shorn sheep, but remember: trees outlive us all – outlive everything. Its legendary predecessor watched cricket's earliest protagonists – Mynn, Pilch, Grace – and then as the twentieth century dawned, and the winter snow came and went every year, was still there to watch Woolley, and Ames, and Cowdrey, and was still there for Knott, Underwood and Denness, and was still there for Benson, Fleming and Key. It was there through uncovered wickets, the first-ever Gillette Cup match, the John Player Sunday League, helmets, pyjama clothing, Durham's first County Championship visit, fielding circles, floodlights, reverse sweeps, Twenty20…

When this new lime tree is finally full-grown and as tall as The Lime Tree that only three players ever managed to hit a six over, what will the game of cricket look like? – and will we even have snow at all by then, or will its branches be bright with Mediterranean bee-eaters and rollers?

DACHA

Here at Worcester College snow has thatched the pavilion, and pleasingly accentuated the white balustrades of the veranda. But whereas during the cricket season the pavilion would be nestling beneath a proscenium arch of green foliage, here the trees are a maze of veins, a madly intricate map of a nervous system. Does that single impending black branch point to something portentous, something amiss? In this icy, skeletal, *Gorky Park* world perhaps it isn't a cricket pavilion at all, but the *dacha* of a Russian police chief.

COLD WAR BATTLEFIELD RELIC

Elsewhere in the former Soviet Union, on a patch of wintry tundra probably littered with discarded shell cases and the beached hulk of an Ekranoplan, we come across this strange piece of abandoned military paraphernalia.
Is it a tank trap, to repel a feared invasion of NATO Patton tanks, or perhaps a rocket launcher?

In fact it's the sightscreen at Aston Rowant cricket ground in Oxfordshire, laid to ground so it doesn't blow over during the winter months.

In February 1954 the actress Dora Bryan
married the Lancashire cricketer Bill Lawton.
As he carried her out of St Thomas's church
in Oldham, someone in the 600-strong
crowd shouted, "Don't drop that catch!"

STROLLING

There is an illicit pleasure in being allowed on the outfield at a cricket ground. Some county grounds don't permit it at all. At others, where you are, invariably some poor oblivious stroller gets barked at by the ground staff for even looking at the square. But in winter snow a cricket ground becomes just white space: a white park. Here at Twickenham Green you can walk where you like. A dog could insouciantly plant a trail of paw-prints right across the smooth white wicket.

❋ Do these walkers even notice there's a sightscreen and a pavilion ahead of them?

✳ Burnsall cricket ground in Wharfedale in the Yorkshire Dales. Just a single pair of feet have mooched down the bank and all the way across to the far boundary.

THE OLD CRICKET FIELD

This cricket ground was transformed long before the snow. It ceased to host matches in 1957 (as is evident from the state of the outfield). This is Wolvey Old Cricket Field Nature Reserve in Warwickshire. The village built a new ground in 1962, and by 1990 the old cricket field, which had returned to cow pasture, had become so swampy that a group of villagers acquired the land as a Millennium project and turned it into a wetland reserve. Barn owls, reed buntings and kingfishers have been seen here, but amid this snowscape two rare, and well-camouflaged, winter visitors are just visible: a pair of cricketers.

ASHLEY HARVEY-WALKER'S TEETH

June 1975 again: only weeks before that inaugural World Cup Final at a sun-drenched Lord's; the same month John Arlott was convinced he'd been snowed on there. But up at Buxton in the Peak District, then a Derbyshire outground, winter came back. The extraordinary County Championship match against Lancashire is memorably brought back to life in the *Wisden Cricketer* anthology *Flying Stumps and Metal Bats*.

On the first day, a gloriously sunny Saturday, Lancs had hit 477, with Clive Lloyd – again – hammering 160, lofting so many straight sixes into the bowling green beyond the ground the bowls there had to be abandoned.

But on the Sunday night a depression moved down from the Arctic bringing very cold air, and on Monday 2 June the Lancashire players woke up at the Railway Hotel to behold snow. No chance of play, and about noon, Jack Simmons recalled later, "It got darker and darker and then for about 20 minutes we were in one of the heaviest snowstorms I'd seen. You couldn't see the other side of the ground." The following day a picture of it appeared in *The Times*, with a confirmation that this was the latest snow had fallen during an English summer since 1888.

By the Tuesday summer had returned, the snow had melted, and play resumed, but the belter of a pitch had become unplayably lethal - Peter Lever refused to bowl fast on it - and Derbyshire were dismissed for 42. After his first ball had reared off a length past his nose their number 5, Ashley Harvey-Walker, handed his false teeth to Dickie Bird for safe-keeping.

"Don't worry, Dickie," he reassured the umpire, who was insisting he wrap them in a hanky first. "I won't be long." Sure enough, a few balls later Harvey-Walker edged one to David Lloyd in the slips. "Did you catch it? You did? Thank God for that." And he collected his teeth, put them back in, and walked off.

SKI RESORTS IN GUYANA

Lancashire's Peter Lever, Clive Lloyd, Frank Hayes and David Lloyd with Dickie Bird at Buxton that Monday morning after play had been called off for the day.

During that lunchtime blizzard, Jack Simmons remembered, Clive Lloyd was "as excited as a kid, running around trying to find a photographer to take pictures of him in the snow."

"I think I'm right in saying there are no ski resorts in Guyana," mused Lloyd, so I had never really seen snow before. I glimpsed it through a window in Moscow one night in '66 when we refueled there on the way to India, but I'd never made a snowball in my own hands.

Lloyd's experience was not unprecedented. "It seems to be the malign fate of West Indies teams to arrive in England in the middle of a cold snap," wrote Learie Constantine in his memoir determinedly titled *Cricket in the Sun*.

It was a blue-faced and shivering mob which stepped thankfully off the boat back in 1939, and once they were here the weather moved steadily back towards mid-winter. I recall practising at the nets a day or so two after the team landed, and snow now began to fall. "What is that?" asked one of the players in an awed voice, watching flakes melting on the hand in which he held the ball.

FOG

Alloa Cricket Club in Scotland, the snow mingling with the winter fog so that the ground seems to be floating beneath the Clackmannan Hills.

Fog – or at least sea-fret – is briefly considered in the principal published work to attempt a meteorological analysis of county cricket, *Rain Stopped Play* by Andrew Hignell, and specifically the assistance it gave at Hove to the swing bowling of Maurice Tate. (In the last county game of the season there a few years ago I watched the sea-mist roll in so densely after tea, that the umpire and non-striker at the Cromwell Road end virtually disappeared from view, and the officials had to have a conversation about suspending play.)

However, it is disappointing to read in *Rain Stopped Play* that, while

there have been occasions, most notably at Buxton in 1975, when solid forms of precipitation, in this case snow, stopped play, … our main concern here is with liquid precipitation, whether it be rain or drizzle.

And that, I'm afraid, is that.

But *Rain Stopped Play*'s chapter on "The Raining County Champions" throws up a mysterious irony. Hignell quotes statistics gathered from a 23-year period between 1946 and 1968 that reveal the wettest county – the county cricket club to have lost most days' play to rain – to be Lancashire, as you'd rather expect, it being so far north and closest to the Pennines. As a rule of thumb, the further west, the worse the weather. And surely snow is just cold-weather rain?

So how come I haven't been able to find a single photograph of Old Trafford covered in snow, or of a single snowy Lancashire League ground? And since the same statistics reveal the driest county to have been Kent, how can there be so many photographs of Tunbridge Wells, and Sevenoaks, and other Kent cricket grounds cloaked in snow?

❄ March 1970, and after the extensive anti-apartheid protests provoked by an earlier Springbok rugby union tour a few months earlier, a forthcoming Test series against South Africa sees the Lord's groundsman taking no chances with the square.

COLOURED CLOTHING

Headingley and the St Lawrence Ground, Canterbury: two examples of why it is so important for all county cricket grounds to install white seating. When it snows, any other colour is thoroughly obtrusive. The new stand at the River Tone end at Taunton (also green) is unfortunate, as are the three rows of electric blue in the upper tier of the (white-painted) pavilion at Hove.

WILLIAM REES-MOGG

In his cricketing memoir, *Shadows on the Grass*, Simon Raven recalls an encounter during his schooldays at Charterhouse with a youthful William Rees-Mogg:

> William was sitting alone, surveying the empty cricket ground with a poetic look. We sat down on either side of him.
>
> "There'th thomething tho forlorn," said William, "about an empty cricket ground."

Raven's friend Conrad, impatient to move on to demolishing Rees-Mogg's contention that copulation invariably gives you syphilis, is not impressed: "What else would you expect it to be in March?"

This is the Upper Ground at Tunbridge Wells, deep in hibernation. Would you agree with Rees-Mogg?

THE SOUTH POLE

Of course, when you find yourself in a landscape where snow is the default element, the perverse urge to play cricket becomes irresistible, at least for Englishmen. This match took place just after the end of the 2006 cricket season – early October, in fact – somewhere in the western Weddell Sea, at a ground that goes by no other name than 64.42°S, 55.18°W.

The expedition from Bangor University's School of Ocean Sciences aboard the icebreaker RV *Polarstern* was in quest of the seldom-visited Larsen B ice shelf on the east coast of the Antarctic peninsula, of intense scientific interest ever since it had disintegrated into thousands of icebergs in 2002. More importantly, according to David Thomas, one of the three cricketers visible in this shot,

Three discarded ice cores provided the stumps, a shovel the bat, and sawed-up 10 cm sections of ice the balls… Bowling a lump of ice is not an easy task, and you certainly know about it if you are LBW when it hits your shins. However, the main problem was that when hit, the "ball" tended to shatter instead of going all the way to the boundary.

Scott's final expedition to the Antarctic faced a similar problem back in 1911 when an attempt to play ice hockey had to be aborted because the puck, made out of shellac and paraffin wax, shattered as soon as struck. His men also had time for many games of 9-a-side football at Cape Evans. But his expedition has gone down in history as an abject failure: not a single over of cricket was bowled.

THE NORTH-WEST PASSAGE

Nearly a century later Harry Thompson, for his cricketing travel book *Penguins Stopped Play,* rectified Scott's omission by staging a brief cricket match at Cape Evans. The bowler wore a bright vermilion cagoule, the wicket was a rucksack, but the ball was a real cricket ball, which a furious skua mistook for an egg when the fielder down at long leg tried to gather it. Then a pod of killer whales surfaced, followed by a humpbacked whale, apparently mesmerised by the action. "Never before," ponders Thompson, "had I seen this many spectators at an amateur cricket match."

Meanwhile, almost a hundred years before Scott's expedition, between 1821 and 1823, at the other end of the earth, William Edward Parry's second voyage went in search of the North-West Passage, and over the winter of 1822-3 his ships were icebound at "Winter Island", Igloolik in northern Canada. This engraving by Edward Finden, from an original drawing by Captain George Francis Lyon, shows Parry's men playing cricket on the pack ice. Boredom and despair during the nine months of confinement were further allayed by Parry's foundation of the Royal Arctic Theatre to stage fortnightly productions.

FIELDING WITH THE BACK OF THE HEAD

Towards the end of the nineteenth century, another game of cricket on ice took place. This time it was in the south of England, at Sheffield Park in Sussex (where the National Trust has recently overseen the reopening of the beautiful, sylvan, and long-closed cricket ground).

This fixture took place on Upper Woman's Way Pond on 17 January 1891, and fortunately the humorist E.V. Lucas (a member of J.M. Barrie's team the Allahakbarries along with Arthur Conan Doyle), wrote a match report for the *West Sussex Times*:

> A. Payne… was faithful to the notion that the best fielding is done on the back of the head… In whatever part of the lake you might be you would be sure to hear a dull thud every few minutes, followed by a peal of laughter…

Harry [Phillips] was one of the few players who wore skates, and though he could skate as well as anyone there, he could not pirouette. Cricket on ice demands pirouetting.

In summer, the bowlers take a run before making their attack; in winter they stand as still as possible, press their knees together and thank heavens if they can get rid of the ball without falling. In summer, the batsmen, in running, just touch the popping crease with the tip of their bats and hurry back again; in winter they shoot a dozen yards past the bowling crease, beat the ice with their feet, plunge their bodies backwards and forwards, and then start for the other wicket. It will be seen that cricket on the ice is more exciting than cricket on the turf.

INZAMAM'S WOOLLY HAT

Cricket on the ice of St Moritz Lake in Switzerland has been played since 1888, and nowadays the Cricket on Ice tournament is contested every February by four teams in a 20-overs round-robin format. There is a matting wicket; the ball is made from hard rubber, and apparently travels further at such rarefied altitude. Tallinn in Estonia is another place where they play ice cricket. The impressive logostyled merchandise of the Cricket on Ice tournament includes a woolly hat, and a Cricket on Ice Mug in which to "enjoy your favourite hot beverage".

The commercial department at Yorkshire CCC might take inspiration: in 2007 Inzamam-ul-Haq's county debut at the Scarborough cricket festival – just before the August bank holiday, mind – was greeted with such bitter cold that the Pakistani Test cricketer took the field wearing a woolly hat, and so numbing was it even in the press box that the *Yorkshire Post*'s cricket correspondent Chris Waters was forced to plunder the club shop for an end-of-season-sale tracksuit and fleece.

ANTIPODES

Australian cricketers, like West Indian, may be utter strangers to snow at their cricket grounds, but not those in New Zealand. This is the club ground at Christchurch on South Island behind the main Queen Elizabeth II Stadium. On 20 April 1930, however, the Australian touring party, on their way across Europe for the forthcoming Ashes series, stepped off the train at Rigi-Kulm in Switzerland to find plenty of snow, and also a member of the Keystone Kops proceeding swiftly in a cricketerly direction. Clarrie Grimmett is far left; Bill Ponsford fourth from left.

❄ Afghanistan's women's cricket team training at the cricket ground in Kabul. For security reasons the "home" venue for international matches is Sharjah in the United Arab Emirates, where there is never a hint of snow.

THE HIGHEST INTERNATIONAL MATCH

There are not many cricket grounds in the world where snow and a full day's play can co-exist. The most amazing has to be the Himchal Pradesh Cricket Association Stadium, at Dharamsala in India up in the Himalayas. Over 1,300 metres (4,200 feet) above sea level (in other words not far short of playing cricket on top of Ben Nevis), with the snow-capped Dauladhar range of hills as the backdrop, it is now generally considered to rival Newlands in Cape Town and the Adelaide Oval for the most picturesque setting for an international cricket ground. Though winter snow had threatened the fixture during the preceding weeks, England played the first-ever one-day international here in January 2013, beating India by 7 wickets. Incidentally (last word on the subject), Himchal Pradesh successfully solves the seat-colour problem by opting for a glorious rainbow profusion across all 23,000 seats.

BEAUTIFUL ENOUGH FOR BRADMAN

No less than Don Bradman *and* Geoffrey Boycott, however, have offered a different, and unexpected, candidate, for most beautiful cricket ground in the world: Brockton Point, in Vancouver.

"The Brockton Point ground is the prettiest upon which it has been my pleasure to play," declared the Don in 1948. "It is really a magnificent setting, and I wish that some of our more important games ... could be played under these ideal circumstances." Boycott played there during an early tour of North America. At the tip of a promontory at the edge of Stanley Park, Vancouver's fabulous swathe of green space, it looks out over English Bay, and back up to the North Shore Mountains enfolding the city. In summer you could go skiing on Grouse Mountain in the morning, play a game of cricket in the afternoon, and have a swim down at the beach in the early evening.

THE HIGHEST GROUND IN THE WORLD?

This picture was taken in the village of Nako (3,712 metres, or over 12,000 feet above sea level), near India's border with Tibet. Cricket reached the community in 1988 when a motor road was built. The dusty cricket ground is an abandoned helipad, and this photograph was taken in 2003 by Romesh Bhattacharji, who visits every three or four years, when children from different alleys were playing each other with home-made cricket bats and tennis balls. Their knowledge of the rules was minimal. Nowadays they have a proper cricket set, and TVs in the village no doubt bring them the IPL.

    Because blustery winds blow most of the time, cricket is played during the three hours or so of calm in the middle of the day. There is no cricket for about four months while the village is snowbound, and then beset with slush after the snow melts. To the right of the pitch is a precipice: any one hitting the ball over it used to be declared out.

NORMAN YARDLEY'S RESIGNATION

"Alas," reflected Anthony Woodhouse of Norman Yardley in his history of Yorkshire CCC, "he should never have been burdened with the politics of Yorkshire cricket in the 1980s." Formerly a distinguished captain of his county, Yardley was considered by some too nice effectively to command a dressing-room of often difficult individuals. A wine merchant outside cricket, he entered the lion's den again on becoming President of the cricket committee in 1981, by which time the club's relationship with Geoff Boycott was becoming strained. Eventually, in 1983, the county decided not to offer Boycott a new contract, which in turn precipitated a vote of no-confidence in the committee. The climbdown early in 1984 that saw him offered a new contract after all was accompanied by several departures from the cricket committee, including Fred Trueman and Yardley.

Here is a dejected Yardley at Headingley immediately after his resignation on 23 January 1984: an elderly man stumbling distractedly away through the snow, clutching his supermarket carrier as though he's just had to clear his desk.

✳ Entangled in frosty tentacles, the roller at Calmore Cricket Club in Hampshire seems not to have moved in years – almost as though it's sunk at the bottom of the ocean.

MISS HAVISHAM

St James Montefiore Cricket Club in Ditchling on the South Downs on
6 April 2008, where the Natwest Bank was organising a "Cricketforce" event
for schoolchildren. The elements decreed that the sporting content of the day
be limited to games of snowballs. The ragged, snow-embroidered nets seem
to have been made from Miss Havisham's wedding dress.

THE FINAL SNOWSTORM

The great cricket writer R.C. Robertson-Glasgow – "Crusoe", as he was known in print - was not painted in monochrome. For this convivial fellow with a "laugh that penetrated all corners of the pavilion", in Alan Ross's words, the best cricket was Festival cricket, capital F, and took place amid "the gay-pennoned tents of some festal ground – Canterbury, or well-nourished Scarborough", and best of all at the seaside, at Weston-super-Mare, or Southend, where he cherished "the saunter from hotel to ground, punctuated by the vinegared whelk and relieved by the esculent cockle". Even cricketers' caps, he felt, should be harlequin-gaudy, and most counties' blues and browns were far too drab: "I like to fancy Hendren in heliotrope and Sutcliffe in sea-green… and the I Zingari cap shines like a beacon in the mist."

Summer, for Robertson-Glasgow, was nothing less than a question of cricketing technique. "I have tried to avoid metaphor and rhapsody," he wrote, "but there was all summer in a stroke by Woolley." Summer was a state of mind: the region of the spirit where the sun is out.

But, like so very many cricketers, Robertson-Glasgow was also depressive, and suffered several breakdowns, and his obituarists make a point of noting that in March 1965 he committed suicide during a snowstorm.

THE POETRY OF SNOW

John Snow, who took 883 wickets for Sussex, and whose record of 25 wickets for England in an Ashes series in Australia in 1971 has never been equalled since, was also a published poet (long hours fielding out on the boundary can only have been conducive to composition), and almost certainly the only cricketer to append the full contents of his two volumes of poems to his autobiography. But while "Have You Been to Pitchpartoo?" does hymn places

> where emerald palms wave frayed arms
> on sands by tropical seas;

Snow's muse does not seem to have contemplated a winter scene like this at the County Ground, Hove.

The last few years of John Snow's Sussex career will have overlapped with the first few of the off-spinner John Childs, who played ten seasons for Gloucestershire before moving to Essex. I wonder if, in one of those Sussex v Gloucestershire County Championship matches between 1974 and 1977, a jocular remark by Childs while bowling to Snow might have goaded the fiery fast bowler into coming down the wicket to hoist the spinner to all parts of the ground? Then the sports pages of the local paper could have run this headline.

**CHILDS SLEDGE MET WITH
SNOW FLURRY**

❋ A snowy cricket ground like West Bretton in Yorkshire looks beautiful to everyone but the groundsman. Snow mould, or fusarium, which enabled Derek Underwood to bowl us to victory in the 1972 Ashes Test at Headingley, can kill the grass and leave circles of brown.

TABULA RASA

One last view of Edgbaston – and on a Sunday morning of shining clarity, 11 April 2008, the newly fallen snow almost tingles with freshness.

In such conditions a cricket ground, and especially this one, is re-made as a blank sheet of white, a *tabula rasa*. How, then, starting from scratch, would one draft that sport of cricket? What kind of things would one leave out to return it to the ideal?

Well, having eradicated colour from cricketers' clothing, how about leaving out all unnecessary aural colour? Here we're looking at an utterly silent world. What should we add back in?

The *clock* of willow against leather, obviously. The strangled holler of an appeal. Applause for a good shot or a departing batsman – that damp patter at a midweek county game; the sea withdrawing down a shingle beach at a packed Test. The murmur of conversation around the boundary – cricket is a sociable spectator sport.

But anything else? The incessant skitter of "Buffalo Soldiers" or "I Want to Break Free" we heard after every wicket, indeed almost every shot, at the 2015 World Cup? Recently I read the Glamorgan captain professing himself pleased, after his side's long day in the field, that "we kept our noise levels up throughout"? Isn't the cricket itself in danger of being drowned out?

A year or so ago Ashley Western, who designed this book, went to the Oval to see a competition for the highest wobbly beer snake, and who could sing "Sweet Caroline" the loudest, or Natwest T20 Blast! to give it its proper name. Eventually the group of ticketholders in front of Ash and his mates had been standing up for so long, obscuring any view of the action, that Ash ventured a, "Do you mind? We can't really see what's going on…" At which point one of the lager drinkers rolled his eyes. "Oh, that's all we need," he exclaimed. *"Cricket fans…"*

MODEST

This is the County Ground at Northampton – one of the most unpretentious and homely places to watch county cricket. The snow confers a softness on this winter scene: if it were a human sensibility it would be mildness, or modesty; an undemonstrative reserve.

In my old BBC cricket videos of '70s Ashes series Geoff Arnold comes in off his stooped run, and delivers a perfect yorker that splays someone like Keith Stackpole's stumps. He stops momentarily to regard the scene of destruction, hands in his pockets - and then he turns on his heel to walk back to his mark. If he really wants to surrender to emotion he might tug out his hanky and blow his nose in an embarrassed fashion.

Even as recently as 1981, there is Bob Willis in his pomp, galloping in at Headingley like a wildebeest and, after Botham's match-turning century, bowling us to improbable victory with the whites of his eyes. His team-mates' jubilation he counters with merely a blank stare that seems to say, "Yeah, so I bowled him?" – before he too trudges off to bowl the next one.

Or there is that 1991 Test, also at Headingley, where, in poor light, amid intermittent rain, on an unpredictable wicket, against the West Indian pace battery of Ambrose, Walsh, Marshall and Patterson, Graham Gooch carried his bat for seven hours to score 154 in what is universally considered to be one of the finest Test centuries of all. And as he brings his hundred up and the whole ground rises in a standing ovation, how does Gooch celebrate? Head down, he simply swishes his bat a couple of times in distracted acknowledgement, before returning to his crease to take guard for the next ball and get on with his innings.

THE HEIGHT OF WINTER

This extraordinary picture, taken at Molesey Cricket Club in Surrey, captures a miraculous, hyper-real winter's day. Those magnificent frosty poplar trees brushing the cotton-wool clouds; a serene white field (could one describe it as whitesward?) on which the white-clad players disport so pleasingly: a day when the slip catches will sting a little, and the fours will probably be all run – but why wouldn't anyone want to play cricket at this time of year?

Except it's actually 23 August 2014, and the height of summer (though almost the same time of year to the day that Inzamam was pulling on his woolly hat against that bitter Scarborough chill), and the photographer Peter Jones has achieved the effect by modifying his camera to allow infra-red light to enter it.

In the *Guardian* last year Toby Chasseaud did note a number of English cricket clubs who make a point of playing in the middle of winter: North Leeds CC on Christmas Day, Brooksbottom CC in Greater Manchester on Boxing Day, and the Lake District villages of Threlkeld and Braithwaite even once playing a winter "Test" on top of Latrigg fell.

He also quotes the author of *Cricket at the Grassroots*, Dick Redbourn, celebrating a Christmas match that was traditionally held in Preston Park in Brighton. When there was snow on the ground, "the most powerful ground stroke … could end up as a snowball on the edge of the square". This was still preferable to playing in warmer temperatures, however, when you would see "the surface churning into liquid mud".

But in each case, snow would appear to be an incidental, not a prerequisite. And if you're merely setting out to play cricket on a rather dank, wintry day, why not just wait for the start of the cricket season?

TIME

This is Ampthill Town cricket club in Bedfordshire. The quietude of this sunset scene has something to do with time seeming to have frozen. And isn't that something to do with the whole point of cricket?

We all love the nailbiting limited-overs finish: four to win off the last ball and the tail-ender's wild swipe, and the ball either slithers to the boundary behind backward point or bowls him neck and crop. But cricket is a long game, and a slow game. Deliciously slow. It takes days. It needs to take days.

A couple of years ago my friend Maddy agreed to come to the cricket with me, so we went to Hove on a lovely sunny day in early June. She sat patiently through the morning session - even asking pertinent questions about why he was standing there, and how was that out – and we had a nice lunch in the beer garden at the Sussex Cricketer and a stroll down to the seafront to look out at the glittering sea, and for the after-lunch session we moved to the deckchairs at the Cromwell Road end, and the scoreboard turned over at a decent three an over, and batsmen came and went. Then, about half an hour after the tea interval, she suddenly said,

"Graham..."
"Yes, Maddy."
"Does cricket *usually* go at this pace...?"

I doubt there's been more than a handful of days of county cricket I've watched (I don't go to shorter formats any more) when there hasn't been at least one moment of suddenly comprehending the sheer *patience*

(a word derived from the Latin verb *patior*, which means to endure, or even to suffer) needed to sit through and assimilate a full day's cricket. Six hours – and even that marks just one slow-motion calving from the iceberg of four days…

The other day – down at Hove again – I watched Sussex take an attritional, inconclusive day not to press home their advantage against Worcestershire, and it would be two more days (when I wasn't there) before the game would swing round and eventually bring them victory. But it needn't have: after four days' play, the whole thing might satisfactorily have ended in a draw.

Isn't it that same daunting feeling you get a couple of hundred pages into a Thomas Mann or George Eliot novel, when there is still three quarters of the book to go, and you know getting to the point where it will have been hugely worth it is going to take so very many more creeping hours of concentration?

WHITE COPPICE

The idyllic cricket ground of White Coppice near Chorley in Lancashire, looking down from Strawberry Bank. It is claimed to be "the most uneven and sloping cricket pitch you will ever see".

The ground was laid out by Mr Ephraim Eccles, who built the local cotton mill, and whose concern for the health of his workers further extended to the provision of a billiards room, and the windows of the factory being left open for the benefits of fresh air. He also ensured the hamlet observed temperance (apparently it still does). The wicket is situated in front of The Row, the terrace of cottages, and runs in line with those toboggan tracks down the hill behind, and you can just spy some of the benches for spectators on the near boundary.

FESTIVAL

The winter sun is about to sink behind the tall terraced houses lining the Trafalgar Square end at North Marine Road, Scarborough. In August, during Yorkshire's festival week, when big crowds will fill the ground to see close neighbours like Durham come to play, the Enclosure at this end will be packed with Yorkshire CCC members, the Tea Room in the top left corner will be doing a non-stop trade in tea and cake, I will be sitting at the far end of these Popular Bank benches with my friends Duncan Hamilton and his wife Mandy, as we do every year, Dickie Bird will be signing autographs on the boundary rope halfway along, and at the opposite end, in the right of shot, a jazz band will be playing beside the marquees during the luncheon interval…

…From the pavilion, past Yorkshire greats like Boycott and Close will be watching. During the tea interval the outfield will be a tangle of miniature games of cricket. Across North Marine Road and beyond the cliff, families are tiny down on the huge sweep of North Bay, scurrying around sandpies or lingering at the water's frilly edge. Back at the cricket, Sidebottom and Brooks will probably be running through the visitors' top order, and then Lyth and Lees getting stuck into their bowlers. Behold the Lord's Test of the north.

And yet, on a hold-your-breath day of gleaming white peace like this, who's to say which is the more beautiful sight?

SOURCES

Flying Stumps and Metal Bats: Cricket's Greatest Moments by the People Who Were There (Aurum, London 2008)

Cricket in the Sun by Learie Constantine (London 1946)

Rain Stopped Play by Andrew Hignell (Frank Cass, London 2002)

Shadows on the Grass by Simon Raven (Frederick Muller 1982, House of Stratus, London 2008)

Penguins Stopped Play by Harry Thompson (John Murray, London 2007)

Cricket in the Park: The Life and Times of Lord Sheffield 1832-1909 by Roger Packham (Methuen, London 2009)

Crusoe on Cricket: The Cricket Writings of R.C. Robertson-Glasgow (Pavilion, London 1985)

Cricket Rebel by John Snow (Hamlyn, London 1976)

PICTURE CREDITS

Merice Ewart Marshall, mericefotografix.com, 1 (Sewerby CC, East Yorkshire)
Chris Stickley, chrisstickleyphotography.com, 2 (Eastcote CC, Middlesex)
PA Images, 5 (The pavilion at Worcester CCC), 29 *left*, 63
Clare Skinner, MCC, 7 (Statue of W.G. Grace, Lord's)
Getty Images, 10, 29 *right*, 64, 74, 76, 90, 91, 100
Graham Morris, Cricketpix, 13, 34, 37
Philip Brown, 14
Alamy, 16, 19, 45, 50, 65
South Essex District Cricket Board, 20
Thomas Nugent, 23
Rex Features, 25, 26 *right*, 87
Mirrorpix, 26 *left*, 33, 49
Tom Rawlings, Warwickshire County Cricket Club, 31
D. Godliman, dgphotos.co.uk, 39
Ted Stebbings, 41
Ady Kerry, 42

John Ward, 46
David Morton, 53
Roger Wickens, Wolvey Environmental Group, 54
Roger Mann Archive, 57, 71, 73
North Notts Newspapers, 59
Thomas Craig, 60
Jonathan Buckwell, 66
Louiza Norman, 69
Darren locomotive-dxc, 77
Andrew Quilty, Oculi, 79
Kunal Narsey, 81
Graham Chapman, 82
Romesh Bhattacharji, 85
David Coombes, 88
Adrian Jones, 92 (Boxmoor CC, Hertfordshire)
Adam Matthews, Sussex CCC, 95
Chris Firth, 96
Ian Yates, 99
Peter Jones, 93
Ampthill Cricket Club, 105
Jeff Worsnop, 106
Allstar Picture Library, 108, 110, 111